Learning Lessons From Furry Friends

by Sarah E. Brown

TEACH Services, Inc.
PUBLISHING
www.TEACHServices.com

World rights reserved. This book or any portion thereof may not be copied or reproduced in any form or manner whatever, except as provided by law, without the written permission of the publisher, except by a reviewer who may quote brief passages in a review.

This book was written to provide truthful information in regard to the subject matter covered. The author assumes full responsibility for the accuracy of all facts and quotations as cited in this book. The opinions expressed in this book are the author's personal views and interpretation of the Bible, Spirit of Prophecy, and/or contemporary authors and do not necessarily reflect those of TEACH Services, Inc.

This book is sold with the understanding that the publisher is not engaged in giving spiritual, legal, medical, or other professional advice. If authoritative advice is needed, the reader should seek the counsel of a competent professional

---

Copyright revised © 2011 TEACH Services, Inc.
ISBN-13: 978-1-57258-726-7 (Paperback)
ISBN-13: 978-1-57258-727-4 (Hardback)
ISBN-13: 978-1-57258-728-1 (E-Book)
Library of Congress Control Number: 2011938899

All scripture quotations, unless otherwise indicated, are taken from the New King James Version®. Copyright © 1982 by Thomas Nelson, Inc. Used by permission. All rights reserved.

Published by

TEACH Services, Inc.
P U B L I S H I N G
www.TEACHServices.com

Dedicated to:
*Hosea, who loves cats,
and Mary Lou, for encouraging me to write.*

In memory of:
*Mama Kitty, Blackie, Smudge, and Tiree—
furry friends sorely missed!*

A special thanks to:
*my mother, for her insight and ideas;
my father and Theodore, for the use of their beautiful photographs;
and most of all, my Heavenly Father—
without Him, none of this would be possible!*

Preface

Dear reader,

These are all true stories. Conversations have been reconstructed, but every event took place. Our family raised kittens for nearly fourteen years—from Mama Kitty (before I was born) to Blackie, who disappeared when I was twelve years old. It was then that we decided to raise puppies. Both experiences brought times of learning, times of sadness and trial, and most of all, times of fun and happiness.

Parents, if you are reading these stories with your children, I would encourage you to look up each verse* in their Bible and help them underline the passage. This will reinforce the messages in their minds and help them to remember the verses later. Some statements have an endnote reference that is listed at the back of the book with a supporting Bible text for you to look up.

Kids, if you are reading this book on your own, good for you! Reading stories that teach you about Jesus helps you develop a better relationship with Him and get ready for heaven. With your parent's permission, underline the Bible promises that are at the end of each chapter and at the end of the book. When you store God's Word in your heart, it's easier to fight against Satan. And if you start when you're young, you'll know a bunch of scriptures when you're older!

It is my hope and prayer that as you read these stories about our furry friends, laughing at their antics and crying through their sorrows, you will feel the Lord's presence and know His immeasurable love, not only for the cuddly companions He blesses us with, but also for you and me.

—Sarah E. Brown

"To everything there is a season, A time for every purpose under heaven" (Ecclesiastes 3:1).

Table of Contents

Chapter 1 The Missing Mama Kitty 7

Chapter 2 The Hidden Kitten 13

Chapter 3 Happy Times—Hard Times 20

Chapter 4 Sarah Picks Puff 29

Chapter 5 Puff's Pumpkin 37

Chapter 6 The Intruder 45

Chapter 7 A New Pet 54

Chapter 8 Puppies 64

Chapter 9 Teaching and Learning 72

The spring sunshine danced merrily on the peeling yellow paint of the old farmhouse.

Chapter 1

The Missing Mama Kitty

Mother was worn out! Baby Sarah was only one week old, and she needed time and attention! Four-year-old Theodore and six-year-old Hosea were as full of energy as any two brothers their age could be. Besides the children, the family pets, puppy Tiree and Mama Kitty—who was soon to be a mother herself—needed care. In addition, the meals needed to be prepared and cleaned up after, the house must be kept in order, and the laundry had to be folded and ironed.

The spring sunshine danced merrily on the peeling yellow paint of the old farmhouse. Inside, Mom busily dust-mopped the kitchen floor, glancing occasionally at the clock. She desperately wished the hands would move faster so Daddy could come home from work to play with the boys, yet at the same time, she hoped they would go slower so that Sarah would nap longer.

"Tell me a story, Mommy, please?" Hosea begged, tired of playing with his Legos.

Mother managed a cheery smile. "About what?"

"Tell me how we got Mama Kitty again."

"Let's see…" Mom paused for a moment to reminisce. "It happened a few years ago during the coldest part of January. I remember hearing a car door slam one afternoon, and I looked out the window just in time to see a strange truck driving off. I didn't think much of it then, but not too long after, little Tiree started barking furiously at something in a tree by the end of the driveway. Finally, I went to investigate, and what do you think I found at the top of the tree?" Mom's eyes twinkled at Hosea.

"Mama Kitty?" he guessed.

"A little kitten; she was so cold she was almost frozen! My, did I have a hard time getting her to come down!" Mother laughed. "I brought her in the house, and we fed her and tried to warm her up, but she was shivering so badly! Her little ears had gotten frostbitten, and eventually the tips fell off. I'm glad I went out there when I did, or she may have frozen to death. It's so sad when people think they can just dump their pets on the roadside when they get tired of them!" Mom sighed and leaned on her mop handle for a moment before resuming her work and her story.

"We adopted her and named her Kitty. Later, after she had had a litter of kittens, we called her Mama Kitty. We actually kept a kitten from one of her first litters. Do you remember Bootsie?"

Hosea nodded. "A little bit. Wasn't she the gray kitty who used to go for walks with us?"

"Yes," Mom laughed. "I don't know of a sweeter kitten yet! She loved to be with us wherever we went. She used to even pad through the snow to go on walks with our family."

"What happened to her?" Hosea wondered.

"Well, one winter she disappeared, and we didn't know where she had gone. When spring came, we found her lying dead by the driveway. We think the snowplow must have hit our sweet little Bootsie. But Mama Kitty soon had more kittens for you boys to play with, even though we didn't keep any of them."

"When will her babies be born this time?" queried Hosea.

The Missing Mama Kitty

We adopted her and named her Kitty.

Learning Lessons From Furry Friends

"I don't know." Mother wrinkled her forehead. "Probably really soon, though. You see," she explained, "a mama cat usually gives birth two months after she gets pregnant. Since we don't know exactly when Mama Kitty got pregnant, we can't set a definite date for her to give birth. We'll just have to keep an eye on her and see." Mom rinsed out her mop and hung it in the closet.

Crunch, crunch, crunch. Mom looked up. "Oh, good, Daddy's home! If you and Theodore finish your chores quickly, maybe he'll push you on the swing! Why don't you feed the pets while Theodore dusts the furniture?"

"OK! Thank you for the story!" Hosea scampered merrily to the enclosed screened porch. He reached for the scooper and filled the doggy's dish and then Mama Kitty's. Tiree immediately began gobbling her food, but Mama Kitty, who usually came running at the first sound of the food rattling in the dish, did not appear.

"Mama Kitty?" Hosea called. "Here kitty-kitty-kitty." He checked inside the doghouse and in a few of Mama Kitty's favorite hiding spots, but nowhere could she be found.

"Mommy, I can't find Mama Kitty!" he wailed.

"Oh, she's probably sleeping in the old barn. Most likely she'll come and eat her food tonight," Mom answered. "If you're finished now, Daddy said he can push you and Theodore on the swing." In a few minutes, she heard the happy laughter outside as Dad pushed the boys on the big swing in the oak tree.

The next morning, however, when the pussy still had not returned, Mom began to worry. "Where could she be?" she wondered aloud.

"You don't think that some wild animal caught her, do you?" Hosea anxiously asked.

"Maybe a coyote or fox ate her!" Theodore said with big eyes.

The Missing Mama Kitty

"Oh, no, I'm sure she's OK," Mom spoke reassuringly. She knew she had to get their minds onto something else. "Would you two like to help me plant the onions in the garden?"

"Oh, can we?" the boys asked excitedly.

"Of course!" Mom laughed. "There's a small paper sack of onion bulbs by the doorway in the porch. "There's not very many onions, but there should be enough to plant at least one row in the garden."

Mom helped the boys tie their shoes, and after putting on her own, she reached for the small sack of onions. She suddenly stopped, her hand in midair. Had she seen the bag move? She lifted the corner and peered inside. What she saw caused her to gasp in surprise. There, curled up in the midst of the onions, lay Mama Kitty! But that's not all—snuggled against her were five of the cutest kittens, not more than a day old!

"Oh, Mama Kitty! What a place to have your babies!" Mom shook her head in pity. "We can't leave you here, that's for sure!" She stroked the new mother on the head and then stood up. "Hosea, please bring me one of the empty fruit boxes from the basement, and Theodore, you can help me find some soft rags to put in the box."

Mother fixed a cozy nest in the box and soon transferred the little family to their new bed. Then she and the boys stood gazing at the sweet little kittens, all of which were busily suckling the warm milk from their mother.

"You know, boys," Mom suddenly remarked, "I think there are some lessons we can learn from this experience. We really should have been watching closer and taking notice of the signs that Mama Kitty would soon give birth. The first sign was that her tummy had grown enormous with all her kittens inside. Also, she has been eating so much food lately that we should have realized it wasn't only for herself but also to nourish all five of her little ones. If we had been paying more attention, we could have prepared a box for her to have her babies in ahead of time. But we were so busy with baby Sarah and all the chores that needed to be done around the house, and she had to find her own quiet place.

"All this reminds me of something in the Bible," Mom continued. "We are told that no one knows the day nor the hour of Jesus' second coming. Then the verse goes on to say that we should watch and pray in case that day should come and we aren't ready![1] Christ gave us many signs that tell of His soon coming.[2] These are what we need to be watching for—just like we should have been watching Mama Kitty's signs.

"Then there is prayer. We need to ask for forgiveness for our sins and give our hearts to the Lord. We should live each day, not for our selfish wishes, but instead for what Jesus wants. In this way, we will always be prepared for Him to come—just as we should have prepared a box for Mama Kitty," Mom explained to the two attentive boys. "We don't want to be so caught up in the cares of this world that we are surprised[3] when Jesus comes, just like we were surprised by the kittens!"

Mom smiled down at Hosea and Theodore. "We want to be ready for Jesus to come, don't we? And we know that He will come very soon, so let's be watching and praying as if He were coming today!"

The boys nodded their heads solemnly. They each gave Mama Kitty one last loving pat before following Mother out to the garden to plant the onions. Mama Kitty thoroughly licked all five of her kittens, loudly and proudly purring over each one, and then she tucked herself around them and fell fast asleep.

"Watch therefore, for you know neither the day nor the hour in which the Son of Man is coming" (Matthew 25:13).

Chapter 2

The Hidden Kitten

"Here kitty-kitty-kitty," called Mom, as she stepped into the porch with a dish of warm cereal. Five little balls of fluff scrambled over the side of the box and scampered to meet her. Mama Kitty placidly rubbed against Mom's leg as she placed the meal on the floor. It didn't take long for the delicious, warm oatmeal to disappear!

"How old are the kitties now, Mommy?" wondered Hosea, trailing after her.

"It's been five weeks since Mama Kitty had them in the onion bag," Mom answered. "Her kittens have grown so fast that it's hard to believe they will soon have to go to new homes!" Mom mused.

Hosea's face fell. "I don't want them to leave!" he whispered.

"I know, Sweetie!" Mother hugged him close. "But don't you remember that you and Theodore get to keep one? Daddy and I decided that the other day. Which one do you think you would like for a pet?"

A sunny smile immediately chased away the rain clouds as Hosea pointed to a mostly-black,

Learning Lessons From Furry Friends

Which one do you think you would like for a pet?

tortoise-shell-colored kitten. "That one! We could call her Blackie."

"Oh, that's a perfect name! She'll keep you happy after the other kittens have to leave. Besides," she continued, "she looks like she could be a good mouser, and that's exactly what we need around here!"

You see, the Browns were not the only ones living in the old farmhouse. Mice had also made it their home. Daddy had set baited traps in dark corners of the cupboards in hopes of reducing the rodent population, but despite the many unfortunate mice who did get caught, more kept moving in! Yes, Blackie would be just the solution to the

The Hidden Kitten

problem—that is, if she really liked mice.

The Browns didn't have long to wait before they found out. One morning Dad quickly checked the mouse traps as usual. "Caught another mouse today," he remarked to Mom. "I guess I had better get rid of it."

"Wait," Mom exclaimed, "I've got an idea! Why not give it to the kittens and see what they do with it?"

So Dad walked outside, calling, "Kitty-kitties! Come see what I brought you."

What happened next was stunning. Just as he bent over to unhook the dead mouse from the trap, little five-week-old Blackie excitedly leapt through the air, grabbed the mouse right out of the trap, and scrambled off with it as fast as she could go! Dad just stood there with the empty trap in his hand and his mouth hanging open in amazement!

From that day forward, Daddy, who hadn't been completely reconciled to having another cat around, willingly welcomed Blackie into the family—that is, just so long as she wasn't brought into the house. "Animals belong outside," he would always say. "They are born with their own fur coats! Besides, they can always sleep in the porch if it's very cold out. So, no pets—not even Tiree, Mama Kitty, or Blackie—in the house!" He spoke firmly, looking straight at Hosea and Theodore, who slowly nodded their heads.

Every year the Browns visited their grandparents up north for Thanksgiving. This time they would be gone for three days. So the family began to busily pack suitcases, sleeping bags, and pillows into the back of the car. Amidst the flurry of activity, one of the boys quietly snuck Blackie into the spare bedroom.

"No one will find me here," he assured himself.

However, he had only played with Blackie for a few minutes when he heard footsteps coming down the hall toward the room. He quickly looked for a place to hide the kitten, and spying the empty dresser in the corner of the room, he stuffed her inside one of the drawers and shut it almost all the way just before Mom opened the door.

"All ready to go, honey? Daddy has the car almost packed. Do you have everything you need for the trip—your suitcase, toothbrush, and pillow?"

"Yes," he answered, trying not to look guilty.

"Then, I would like it if you would come in the kitchen and help me finish making sandwiches for supper," she instructed, as she turned to leave the room.

He followed, peeking quickly into the drawer as he went by. Blackie had snuggled up in one corner of the drawer. He had no time to put her back outside now without being seen. She was content for now, and he felt sure he could put her outside later.

But when that task was done, Mom asked both boys to help her tidy the house, and then to help prepare a quick lunch to eat before they left. After that, the dishes needed to be washed, and almost before he knew it, they were on their way. The excitement of traveling soon pushed

The Hidden Kitten

aside all thoughts of the little kitten sleeping in the dresser drawer.

Three days later the car pulled into the driveway, and everyone piled out, sad that their trip had ended, yet happy to be home again. Mother and Daddy began directing Hosea and Theodore as to which things to carry into the house.

Mom, with the boys' suitcases and pillows in her arms, headed upstairs to deposit her load. She set the pile on the bed and had just turned to leave when she heard a mournful sound. She stood still and listened for a moment. Maybe her imagination was playing tricks on her—but, no, there it was again: a loud and pitiful *meow*, and it sounded

as though it was coming from the spare bedroom downstairs. Mom hurried to the room and, following the sound, quickly pulled open the partially-closed drawer. What a sight met her eyes!

"Blackie!" she gasped. "You poor, little kitty! You must have been in this drawer the whole time we were gone!" she cried in amazement. "You're almost starved, and I'm sure you're dying of thirst—poor thing!" She gently scooped the weak and bedraggled kitten out of the drawer and carried her to the kitchen. She gave Blackie a dish of water and food, and the little kitten ate and drank until her little tummy bulged out like a balloon. It wasn't until then that she was finally satisfied.

Then Mother called both boys and asked for an explanation. The culprit hung his head and whispered the story of how he had brought the kitten inside and hid her so he wouldn't be caught disobeying. Mom took him on her lap and soberly explained to him, "Honey, little

Blackie could have died without food or water like that. If we had been gone one more day, we probably would have been too late to save her!

"You know," she went on, "the Bible says, 'Be sure your sin will find you out.'⁴ You knew that Daddy did not want the kitty in the house, so you snuck her in while no one was watching. But God is always watching us, and there is nothing we can hide from Him! Whenever we disobey, someone has to suffer because of it, just like Blackie had to suffer for your mistake. Now, let's take Blackie outside to her mother, shall we?"

But, to their surprise, Mama Kitty warily eyed her meowing kitten with disdain. When Blackie tried to get close to her, she slapped her away with a snarl.

Mom picked up Blackie and cuddled her in her arms. "Poor kitty, your Mama doesn't recognize you after being apart for three days," she crooned, stroking Blackie's soft fur. "Your smell is probably different

now. But you'll be fine, since you're almost old enough to be weaned

The Hidden Kitten

anyway." Mom set the kitten on the ground, and the little ball of fur waddled away to her favorite spot in the sunshine and curled up to take a nap.

Later that evening for family worship Daddy read from Genesis 3 about Adam and Eve eating the forbidden fruit. "They ran and hid, too, when they heard God coming," he explained after he had finished reading. "God had told them they would have to die if they ate of the fruit, but because He loved them so much, He sent His Son, Jesus, to be punished in their place.

"Jesus was born and lived a perfect, sinless life here on earth, but when He was grown, wicked men who hated Him had Him crucified. Yet He rose back to life on the third day—just like we came home and rescued Blackie after three days. In this way, He died the death we should die, just because He loves us!"[5]

Mom put her arms around both boys and concluded, "Always remember what terrible suffering comes because of one sin that seems so small. You must say 'no' to Satan's temptations and be obedient to Christ and your parents instead. Then you will make Jesus happy!"[6]

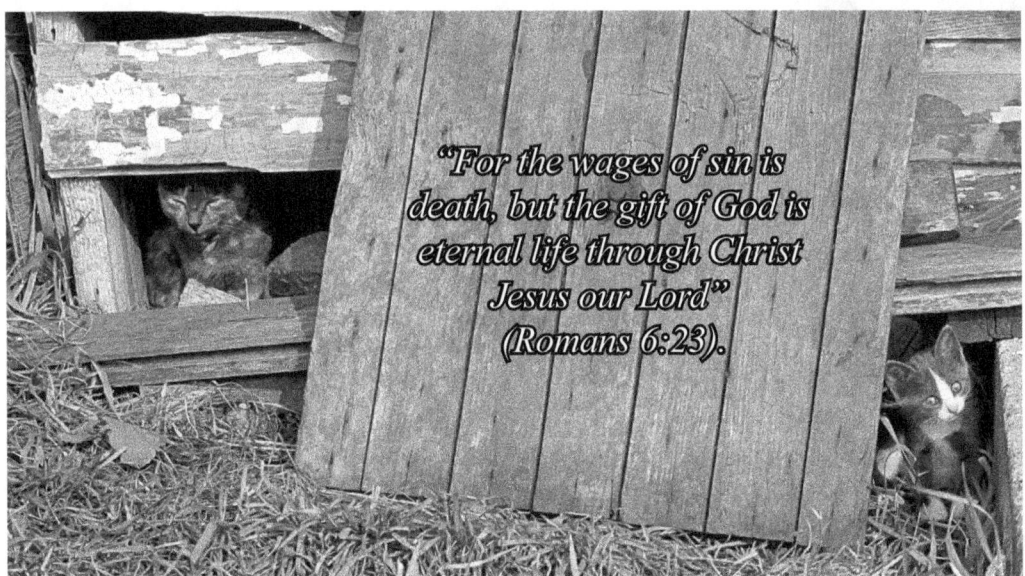

"For the wages of sin is death, but the gift of God is eternal life through Christ Jesus our Lord" (Romans 6:23).

Chapter 3

Happy Times—Hard Times

Time passed quickly, and soon all Blackie's brothers and sisters had gone to new homes. Blackie herself grew more mature each day. She was indeed an excellent mouser, and she soon had the pests under control.

Sarah had grown as well. Now nine months old, she could pull herself up to a standing position while holding onto a bench or chair. She even walked around the house pushing a red, plastic stool in front of her. The linoleum suffered, but Sarah soon learned to walk on her own. She enjoyed babbling and making all sorts of baby noises.

One day Mom walked into the kitchen where Hosea and Theodore were playing with Sarah. She watched as Sarah clutched the windowsill and pulled herself up to look outside. At that moment, Mama Kitty jumped onto the doghouse, which was situated under the window outside. Sarah saw her and said, "Kitty!" just as clear as could be!

Mom was astonished. "Sarah's first word is kitty! Let's write it down on the calendar!'" With excitement only a mother can know, Mom penciled the news under the date. "We'll definitely have something to tell Daddy when he comes home!" she said as she picked up her daughter and gave her a loving squeeze.

The boys could hardly wait for Daddy to come home to tell him. "Maybe she'll be one of those early talkers that you wish had never learned how," Dad teased. But months passed by before Sarah spoke again.

More happy news came. Hosea and Theodore could hardly contain their excitement when Mom told them that Blackie was pregnant and would have a batch of kittens.

"I can hardly wait to play with her little kitties!" Hosea exclaimed.

"Should we make her a box to have them in?" Theodore wondered.

"I don't think we'll need to this time," Mom decided. "Since we have the horses now, she can sleep in the hay shed. She'll nestle down into the hay and be warm and safe with her kittens."

The boys patiently counted the days until the appointed time for Blackie to give birth. One day, as the time neared, Hosea noticed that Blackie hadn't appeared for her meal as she usually did. So Mother, Hosea, and Theodore hurried to the hay shed to see if she had had her kittens.

"Now, remember to be very quiet," Mom cautioned as they approached the shed. "Mother cats don't like to be bothered by loud commotion when they have newborn kittens," she explained in a whisper. "If we make too much noise, Blackie might get upset and hide her kittens where we can't find them. Then they would grow up wild and scared of people. We don't want that, do we? We want them to be friendly kitties."

The boys nodded silently. Mom pulled open the shed door, and sure enough, Blackie lay nestled into the loose hay with three kittens snuggled close beside her.

"Oh," Theodore breathed, "Blackie did have her babies!"

"But, Mommy," Hosea whispered, bending close to the little babies, "why do they look funny? Look at their mouths!"

Mom was not smiling anymore. She knelt beside Blackie with a concerned look on her face. Then she stood up and took the boys hands. "Let's go back to the house," she spoke softly, leading them out of the shed and closing the door. "I'll explain what's wrong then."

Back inside, Mom took Theodore on her lap and Hosea sat next to her on the couch. Mom took a deep breath. "Sweethearts, the little kitties probably won't live very long."

"But why, Mommy?" they cried.

"Remember how their mouths looked funny? Well, they have cleft pallets, which means that the roof of the mouth is split. You may not completely understand that now, but it makes it impossible for them to nurse and get the milk they need from their mommy. Without proper food, the kittens will just get weaker and weaker until they fall asleep and die. I'm sorry." As Mom hugged the sobbing boys, tears slid down her own cheeks as well.

In a few days the three little babies were gone. "I'm so sorry, boys! But cheer up. There will be more kittens soon," Mom said, trying to comfort Hosea and Theodore.

Blackie and Mama Kitty did indeed have more babies, and as time rolled happily by, the family forgot about the death of Blackie's first kittens. Besides, everyone was busy packing for another trip that summer. This time they weren't just leaving for three days—they were moving! All the household items had to be packed into boxes, ready for the big day.

Three-year-old Sarah tried her best to be helpful, but she usually only got in the way and made things harder for everyone. Seven-year-old Theodore and nine-year-old Hosea thought for sure that moving day would never come, but at last the day arrived.

Most of the furniture and large, heavy belongings had been packed into a trailer, while the smaller items were packed into the family car. Daddy, Mother, and Sarah sat up front, and Hosea, Theodore, and the box containing Mama Kitty and Blackie sat in back. Tiree lay curled at the boys' feet. The two horses were transported in yet another trailer.

As the car pulled out of the driveway, everyone gazed one last time on the old home they were leaving.

"I'll miss playing in the barn," Hosea said.

"Yes, the farm was nice," Mother spoke with a smile, "but I certainly won't miss all the mice and bats that lived in the old house!"

"Our new house will be much better," Dad put in. "We can thank the Lord for providing such a nice country home to move to."

"Do you think Mama Kitty, Blackie, and Tiree will like our new place?" Theodore wondered.

"Oh, they probably won't understand at first that we are going to live somewhere else, but they'll soon adjust and grow to like their new home," Mom answered.

Soon the car turned off the main road onto a dead-end gravel lane, and it wasn't long before the Browns spotted the light-blue Rambler situated on a small hill. Fields of corn and soybeans surrounded the wooded yard, which was large enough for a big garden and had plenty of space to play.

Learning Lessons From Furry Friends

...the Browns spotted the light-blue Rambler situated on a small hill.

Now the unpacking occupied everyone's attention. The house that had seemed so large on arrival now seemed to be crowded with boxes and furniture. Many weeks passed before the family finally felt settled.

Winter had almost arrived when the boys found that Mama Kitty was soon to have another litter of kittens. She decided to make her nest in a cozy pile of hay that was covered with a tarp out in the yard. It wasn't long before she was the proud mother of a small family of adorable kittens.

Blackie was also pregnant, but for some reason no one noticed until one day Theodore hurried inside with a troubled look on his face. "I haven't seen Blackie for a while. I don't know where she is!" he wailed.

"Oh no! Let's keep our eyes open for her. Maybe she's just hiding somewhere," Mom reasoned.

Blackie was hiding! Thankfully, Mom happened to notice her crawling under a red shed near the house. "I wonder..." Mom began, and then, taking a flashlight, she knelt down and shone it under the shed. Sure enough, there lay Blackie with a litter of kittens!

"Oh, Blackie!" Mom exclaimed, almost in exasperation. "I didn't even know you were pregnant! Couldn't you have picked a better place to have your babies, though? At least they look healthy. Well, let's see if I can reach you, and I'll find a nice box to put you and your babies in," Mom told Blackie. But even though she reached under the shed as far as she could, the kittens were too far out of her grasp.

That night the temperatures dropped, and a freezing wind began to blow. The next morning frost coated everything outside. Mom hoped and prayed that the kittens had survived the night, but of course, there was nothing she could have done for them, since she couldn't reach them the day before.

The poor little kitties froze that night, and later on Mother found them lying dead on the lawn where Blackie had dragged them. But that wasn't the end of the sadness, for almost in the same week Mama Kitty's litter of beautiful babies disappeared. When Mom searched through the nest in the hay, she found telltale signs that the tomcat had come in the night and killed them.

Hosea and Theodore were heartbroken that the little kittens were gone all at the same time. "The naughty, naughty tomcat!" Theodore sobbed.

"We must understand that animals are not like people," Mom explained. "Remember how Blackie dragged her dead kittens out on the lawn? She no longer thought of them as her children whom she loved, but just as dead 'things' that would soon decay. She naturally wanted to get rid of them, so she dragged them out of her sleeping area. In the same way, the tomcat didn't think of the kittens as his own children but as intruders or threats to his territory."

"But Blackie should have known better than to have her kitties under the shed!" Hosea cried.

Learning Lessons From Furry Friends

"Oh, Sweetheart, it is actually quite normal for a mother cat to be inexperienced when she first starts having kittens. She'll give birth in strange places—like under a shed where her kittens can't keep warm—and sometimes she won't take care of them or feed them properly. But the more litters she has, the more sense she will develop in those matters. You just wait, Blackie will have a lovely, healthy batch of kittens yet."

"It seems like something bad happens to all our kitties!" Hosea observed sadly. "I was looking forward to having kittens again, and now they're all dead! Couldn't Jesus have protected them?"

"Yes," Mom replied thoughtfully, "He could have. But remember that Jesus never makes anything bad happen to us. Satan is the one who brings all the evil, death, and sorrow into this world. The Bible says that he walks about like a roaring lion, seeking whom he may devour[7]—sort of like the tomcat.

"But sometimes the Lord *allows* these sad experiences to happen because He knows what is best for us." Mom continued, "We must remember that all things will work together for good if we love God[8]; so even if some situation seems terrible, good will come of it! Perhaps Jesus wants us to learn a valuable lesson from our experience, or maybe He has something better in store for us."

"Maybe sad things happen to people, but why should the awful things happen to such sweet animals?" Hosea wondered.

Mom sighed. "Because of sin. God didn't intend this world to have sorrow and death. The Bible says that He made everything good.[9] But when Adam and Eve disobeyed God, the punishment was death, and since we all have sinned, we all have to experience pain and death[10]—even the animals. After sin came to the earth, the animals changed. They began to kill and fight and hurt.

"But we know that someday soon Jesus will come again and wipe away all our tears, and 'there shall be no more death, nor sorrow, nor crying. There shall be no more pain.'"[11] Then all the animals will live together in peace and happiness, and they won't kill or hurt each other anymore!"[12]

"I can hardly wait for heaven!" Theodore exclaimed, smiling through his tears.

"Yes, and from now on, we'll always make a box up on a shelf in the garage where no cold weather or tomcats can kill anymore of our kittens," Mom resolved.

Other sad experiences would come to the Brown family and their pets, such as when Mama Kitty mysteriously disappeared forever; but these sad times only caused the family to be more thankful for happy times and look forward to perfect happiness in heaven.

And in the years that followed, the whole family enjoyed many healthy, sweet kittens from Blackie. She usually had four or five kittens each time—oranges, calicoes, blacks, grays, and mixtures of those colors. And so both the family and their cat, Blackie, learned valuable lessons from the hard times.

"'The wolf and the lamb shall feed together ... they shall not hurt nor destroy in all My holy mountain,' says the Lord" (Isaiah 65:25).

Learning Lessons From Furry Friends

...sad times only caused the family to be more thankful for happy times and look forward to perfect happiness in heaven.

Chapter 4

Sarah Picks Puff

"I want a kitty of my own!" six-year-old Sarah declared emphatically at the lunch table one sunny spring afternoon.

"Why do you say that?" Dad asked.

"Because Hosea has Blackie, and Theodore has Tiree, and I want a pet!" she replied.

"Well, we'll have to think about that one!" Daddy never liked to make hasty decisions.

Three years had passed since Mama Kitty had disappeared. Blackie still had a litter of kittens every so often. Now Sarah was old enough to enjoy them too, but she still wished one of them could be her very own.

"Let's let her keep one," Mom suggested to Dad later when they were alone. He wasn't so sure about adding another pet to the family. "But now that we have to find new homes for the horses, she's going to be lonely," Mom reasoned. And so Daddy agreed.

Sarah could hardly wait for another litter to be born so she could pick out a kitten for her very own. Blackie gave birth to five kittens early one morning

Learning Lessons From Furry Friends

...the kittens were soon trying out their wobbly legs.

not long after. Blackie lovingly licked them to dry their fur and help them begin breathing. She nestled close to her babies to keep them warm. She was a very good mother by now.

The little kittens eyes and ears were tightly sealed shut, and they were very weak and helpless. Only a week had passed, however, before Sarah discovered five pairs of wide eyes looking quizzically up at her. She excitedly ran shrieking to the house, "The kitties eyes are open, Mommy!" She soon returned with Mom in tow.

Always full of questions, Sarah asked, "Mommy, why were their eyes shut when they were born?"

Mom smiled. "God wisely planned that at creation. Before they are born, the kittens grow inside their mother's womb, which is like a special room in her tummy. It is very dark and quiet in there. It would be a big shock for them to suddenly be born into our bright and loud world. And so, for the first week, their eyes and ears are closed to keep out the sunshine and the noises until they develop more fully. Over the past few days their eyes and ears have opened slowly, letting in a little more light and sound each day. Now that they can see, they will probably start learning to walk."

True to Mom's prediction, the kittens were soon trying out their wobbly legs. At first they would clumsily stand up, only to fall back again. The exercise strengthened their legs, though, and they grew more agile each day. Hosea, Theodore, and Sarah often came to watch the kitties play. They laughed and giggled as the kittens pounced and tumbled, growling and swatting at their siblings.

It wasn't long before they were crawling over the sides of their box, which was situated on the top of a work table, to explore their surroundings. After they grew tired of playing on top of the table, they crawled into the woodpile next to the table and played in the "tunnels" made between the unevenly stacked logs. When they finally gathered enough courage, they shinnied carefully down the side of the pile to the garage floor to amuse themselves for hours among all the curious-looking things stored there.

One bright morning in June as Sarah and Theodore sat watching the kittens frolic around in the box, Sarah remarked, "You know, Theodore, I like this one best!" She scratched a little gray and white kitten under the chin. "She's the cutest, and I want her to be my very own!" Then Sarah picked her up in her arms and stroked her fur while crooning, "Hey there, cutie! You're such a pretty kitty!"

Theodore picked up a dark-gray calico kitten. "You know what I think?" he asked. "I think Smokey is stronger and tougher than *her!*" He looked critically at the kitten Sarah held. "Why don't you keep Smokey instead? I think you'd be happier with him, and I'm sure he's smarter than a girl kitten anyway!"

Sarah just hugged her kitty all the tighter and retorted, "Maybe *you'd* pick Smokey, but I like…" she thought quickly, "Puff—after the kitty in the Dick and Jane books—best of all." And so she picked her pet.

When the kittens were four weeks old, Sarah found Mom in the kitchen pouring warm milk and water over a pan of cat food. "What are you doing, Mommy?" she wondered.

And so she picked her pet.

Sarah Picks Puff

"The kittens are ready to learn to eat moistened dry food to supplement their mother's milk," Mom explained. "Here, you may carry this outside for me."

When the kittens heard the familiar call of "Here kitty, kitty, kitty" they tumbled out of the box to greet Mom and Sarah. Sarah set the pan on the shelf and the kittens gathered around, fascinated by the new object. They sniffed at the luscious aroma but didn't know how to eat it.

Tiger suddenly decided to see how the new thing tasted and stuck his nose a little too eagerly into the milk, only to come up sputtering and sneezing. Mom and Sarah laughed, and then gently stuck all the kitten's noses into the milk. They licked their noses off, and, *oh*, the taste was so good! Puff tried to gulp a mouthful but only came up sputtering just like Tiger.

Blackie, who must have been out hunting, came running just then, meowing for the food. She jumped onto the shelf and began to lap up the milk and cat food. "See, Sarah, the kittens will watch their mother and learn how to eat from her," Mom pointed out. Following Blackie's example, the kittens' tummies were soon bulging with the warm food.

Then Mom and Sarah put each of the kittens into the litter box. "Hold the kitten's front paws, and make scratching motions with them," Mom instructed. Sarah took Puff's front paws and helped her dig a hole into the kitty litter. "The kittens will think it's strange at

Learning Lessons From Furry Friends

first, but they will soon understand that it's very important to use the litter box after they eat."

Sarah had so much fun in the weeks that followed! She would bring a few kittens into her bedroom at a time, tie a yarn ball to the light fixture on the ceiling with a long string, and spend hours watching the kittens scramble after the ball as it swung in a wide circle. Sarah never grew tired of watching them play!

Another favorite activity was making kitten-houses. Hosea and Sarah made them from cardboard boxes glued together with lots of doorways, tunnels, secret passages, and peepholes. The "houses" even had "stairs" (made from strips of old towels glued to the sides of the boxes) leading to the upper levels. The kittens spent many happy hours scrambling and hiding, pouncing and playing in these houses. Puff amused herself there after her brothers and sisters had gone to new homes.

Sarah never grew tired of watching them play!

Sarah Picks Puff

One day Sarah made a grave mistake. She carried Puff up into a tall tree and tried to get her to jump down from a high branch. She pushed from behind, but the kitty, scared of the great distance to the ground, dug her claws in. One push too hard, and suddenly Puff was falling. *Thump*! Blood oozed from a painful cut on her lip. She had fallen onto a tree root sticking out of the ground.

Sarah saw the blood and started to scream. Mother came running from the house. "What happened, what happened?" she called. She gently picked Puff up while, between sobs, Sarah told the story.

After Mom cleaned the wound, she took Sarah onto her lap. "Sarah," she said in a serious voice, "that was a very foolish and dangerous thing to do."

Sarah began to cry again. "Blackie climbs trees and jumps down," she sniffled. "I thought Puff would be able to."

"But, you see, Puff is just a little kitten, like a baby, and she's much too small to jump that far. When she is older and bigger, she'll be able to jump farther."

"Is she going to die?"

"No, she isn't going to die, but she has badly cut her lip, and I'm afraid it will be sore for quite a while. She'll probably have trouble eating as well."

"I'm sorry, I didn't know!" Sarah said soberly.

"The Bible says that not even one little sparrow falls to the ground without the Father in heaven seeing.[13] I'm sure He was watching over your kitten. Maybe He allowed this to happen to help you learn a lesson. The Bible also says, 'Do not fear therefore; you are of more value than many sparrows.'[14] If God even takes notice of the little birdies and kitties that fall, just think how much He loves you!

"Some people think that God is always angry and waiting to strike them down for making any little mistake. Nothing could be further from the truth! He tells us in the Bible that 'I have loved you with an everlasting love.'[15] Yes, He loved us so much that He sent His only Son to die for our sins.

"There is a time," Mom continued, "when the Father is angry. He wouldn't be a loving God if He *wasn't* moved to anger when those He loves are hurt, hated, and harmed. But His anger is toward *sin* and not the *sinner*. The Bible says, 'But God demonstrates His own love toward us, in that while we were still sinners, Christ died for us.'[16] What a loving God we have!"

Sarah nodded, wiping the tears from her cheeks, and managed a smile.

"Now, Puff is going to be fine." Mom lifted Sarah off her lap and put the kitten in her arms. "Why don't you take her outside to her box."

For a few days, Puff's lip *was* quite sore, and she ate very little. By and by, however, the cut healed, but it left her lip misshapen, causing her to drool at times and serving as a reminder to Sarah of the important lesson she learned that day.

"For God so loved the world that He gave His only begotten Son, that whoever believes in Him should not perish but have everlasting life" (John 3:16).

Chapter 5

Puff's Pumpkin

When Puff was almost a year old, she had her first batch of kittens! However, it wasn't long before the Browns discovered that she was not a very good mother either. No, she didn't hide her kittens under sheds, but she didn't seem to want to feed them and take care of them. "She even makes Blackie nurse her babies, besides Blackie's own kittens!" Hosea exclaimed to Mother.

"Well, young cats sometimes aren't very wise with their first few litters. Remember how Blackie was? And now she is a very good mother! Puff just needs experience and time, that's all. We'll have to make sure that her kittens are getting enough food," Mom answered.

"It's a good thing that Blackie had her kittens a few days before Puff! Blackie is such a good mother that she doesn't seem to mind feeding all the kittens," Hosea laughed.

Puff's kittens managed to get their share of the nourishing milk from Blackie, and since it wasn't long before they were eating moistened dry food, they grew up to be fat and healthy. With two litters of kittens, there seemed to be kitties everywhere. "Five kittens from Puff and five from Blackie is just too many!" Dad declared emphatically.

And so, soon after all the kittens had gone to new homes, Mom, Hosea, Theodore, and Sarah put Puff in a box, folded the lid shut, and put the box in the car. "Hold the lid down so Puff can't get out," Mom told Sarah. They were taking Puff to the vet to be spayed.

Learning Lessons From Furry Friends

"Puff just needs experience and time, that's all."

"If Puff could talk, she'd probably say that cars are dreadfully fearful places," Theodore said. "She'd wonder why we would ever want to ride in them," he laughed.

"Mommy, what's spaying? It won't hurt Puff, will it?" Sarah asked.

"Spaying is when the vet takes out a female cat's reproductive organs so that she can't have kittens," Mom answered. "The vet will have to cut her open on her tummy, but don't worry; it won't hurt her. The vet will give her a shot that will make her sleep, and she won't feel a thing. When he's done, he'll sew up the cut with a special needle and thread. When Puff wakes up later, she'll probably feel stiff and sore, but it won't take long for that to mend."

"But Mommy," Sarah wailed, "why do we have to spay my poor, little Puff? I want her to have more kittens!"

"Now, Sarah," Mom quieted her, "you know how Daddy feels about having so many kittens running around! Besides, Blackie will still have more babies." Mom tried to console Sarah.

Just then, Puff succeeded in pushing open the box and scrambling up onto a seat. She meowed piteously. "Hey Puff-kitty, don't be scared. It's OK! Come here and I'll pet you," Sarah implored, reaching for her. But Puff didn't want to be petted! *She wanted out!* She scratched and bit and fought until Hosea caught and held her in a towel.

She finally calmed in his arms. But as soon as the car rolled to a stop, she clambered for the door. Mom quickly caught her, put her back into the box, and carried it into the veterinary office.

Mom talked briefly to the lady at the desk and then signed some papers. Then she opened the box and quickly caught Puff before she could scramble to the door. "Here she is," Mom said. "Now you be good, Puff!"

"Goodbye poor, little Puff!" Sarah whispered while Hosea stroked her fur and Theodore scratched her under the chin. Then they walked out the door and were gone. The lady put Puff into a cage where she soon she fell fast asleep.

When Puff awoke, the vet was talking to the lady. The lady took her out of the cage and laid her on a table. Puff struggled to get away from the strangers, but the lady held her firmly. The vet then quickly gave Puff a shot with a big needle. *Ouch!* that needle hurt! But then everything went numb, and Puff fell sound asleep again.

The next morning the lady called Mom to let her know that Puff was doing fine and could come home. When Mom and the children arrived at the veterinary office, they found Puff still asleep, so they gently picked her up and carried her to the car.

"When will she wake up?" Sarah wondered.

"I'm not sure." Mom wrinkled her forehead. "But she'll need to rest quietly for the rest of today and probably tomorrow. We'll put her on the couch in the house, and then we'll go to town and do some shopping."

When Puff finally woke up, no one was home. She tried to stand up but felt very dizzy and plopped to the floor. She felt so funny; everything in the room seemed to be spinning, and when she tried to walk, the floor seemed to wobble beneath her. The shot the vet had given her to make her sleep during the surgery was making Puff feel very strange.

Soon Daddy arrived home from work, and seeing Puff in her condition, he quickly confined her to a box where she wouldn't fall and hurt herself. When Mom and the children returned from town, Puff was feeling much better, and the dizziness of the shot was wearing off.

Sarah took her kitty on her lap and stroked her gently. She turned her carefully on her side and gazed at her tummy. "Mom," she called in a perplexed voice, "you said the vet would sew up the cut, but I don't see a cut or any stitches!"

"They must be there, Sarah. Maybe you aren't looking in the right place." Mom came over to take a look. "Here's where the vet shaved Puff's fur away, but that's funny, I don't see a cut or any stitches either! They must be too small to see," Mother concluded.

But it wasn't too long before it became quite obvious that Puff was pregnant! A very bewildered Mom called the vet right away.

"Guess what!" she exclaimed to the family after hanging up the phone. "They said they didn't spay Puff after all! I guess she was already pregnant when we brought her in, and the vet found out after he had given her the shot. Somehow his secretary hadn't been informed, and so when I picked Puff up afterward, she told me that Puff *had* been spayed! What a mix-up!" Mom laughed.

Soon after, Puff gave birth to her second batch of kittens. "Maybe Puff will be a better mother this time," Sarah hoped.

However, unbeknownst to anyone, even if Puff did want to care for her babies, she found it very hard to get into her box to do so. You see, the children had made her a new box, but they had accidentally made the opening too small. She couldn't get inside very well to feed her kittens or sleep with them when the nights turned cold. When Mom finally realized it, the poor little kittens were getting very weak and hungry. She quickly brought them into the house, put them in an open box on a heating pad, and set Puff in the box with them to feed them.

All the kittens quickly revived except one little orange one who couldn't seem to pull through. Soon little Pumpkin was very cold and too weak to drink the nourishing milk from his mother. Mom tried feeding him warm, watered-down cow's milk with a teaspoon, but her efforts were in vain. Pumpkin went to sleep for the last time in Mom's arms late one night.

Learning Lessons From Furry Friends

Pumpkin went to sleep for the last time in Mom's arms late one night.

When Sarah woke up the next morning, Mom had to tell her the sad news. Sarah began to cry, "Why, Mommy, why?" she sobbed.

Mom took her in her arms and silently rocked her back and forth. Finally, she spoke, "A long time ago, Sweetheart, there was a good and righteous man whom the Lord had richly blessed. He had a lovely wife, lots of children, and many herds and flocks of animals. His name was Job. Satan hated this godly man, and he asked God if he could make Job's life miserable, and then 'he will curse You to Your face,' Satan told the Lord.

"So the Lord gave Satan permission to afflict Job, and one day servants came running to tell Job that all his children and all his flocks and animals had been killed. You can imagine how sad that would have made poor Job! Even his wife told him to curse God. But Job did something else instead. He said, 'The Lord gave, and the Lord has taken away; blessed be the name of the Lord.'[17]

"And do you know what happened at the end of the story?" Mom asked. "The Lord gave back to Job many, many times more and even better than what he had before—cattle, sheep, camels, and many beautiful children!"

"Really?" Sarah's eyes opened wide.

"He surely did!" Mom hugged Sarah close. "Bad things will happen to us in life, but let's always remember what Job did, and let's praise the Lord and thank Him that He always does what's best! Then, instead of being sad, we can be happy and think of all the fun times we have had with our kittens and look forward to having more litters!"

Sarah nodded with a smile; then her face sobered again. "Poor Pumpkin! What is it like to die?" she asked.

"The Bible tells us that death is like a sleep.[18] When you are asleep, you don't know anything until morning, when you wake up. It's the same way with death. If you die, you won't know anything until the resurrection morning.[19] When Jesus calls you out of the grave, He'll take you and all those who love Him to heaven to be with Him forevermore!"

"Mommy, will Pumpkin be in heaven?"

"That's hard to know." Mom gently stroked Sarah's hair and thought for a moment. "The Bible never says anything about Jesus bringing our pets to heaven, but we do know that there will certainly be many animals there. It could be that when Jesus comes again, He will put little Pumpkin in your arms and you can spend the rest of eternity with him! But until then, he will just sleep quietly without any more pain."

That day the family buried little Pumpkin close to the house, but their sadness was turned to joy at the thought of what Jesus had in store for the future.

"But I do not want you to be ignorant, brethren, concerning those who have fallen asleep, lest you sorrow as others who have no hope.... For the Lord Himself will descend from heaven with a shout, with the voice of an archangel, and with the trumpet of God. And the dead in Christ will rise first. Then we who are alive and remain shall be caught up together with them in the clouds to meet the Lord in the air. And thus we shall always be with the Lord"
(1 Thessalonians 4:13-17).

Chapter 6

The Intruder

Soon after the kittens went to new homes, the Browns again took Puff to the vet to actually get spayed. Next spring Blackie gave birth to another batch of kittens. Puff had obviously lost all her mothering instincts. When the kittens were first born, it was easy to keep her distance from them, but it didn't take long before they were scampering all over the place. Everywhere she went there always seemed to be kittens following her and trying to play with her!

One day Sarah remarked to Mom, "Puff is mean to Blackie's kittens! She hisses at them, and the other day I even saw her swat one in the face!"

"Since Puff is spayed now, she doesn't have the hormones that give her feelings of love toward babies. Instead she looks on them as another animal coming into her territory, and she is jealous of them. God did not plan for animals to love the way humans do. Even if people don't have children, they can still love other children," Mom said.

"And Jesus loves us no matter what!" Sarah added.

"Yes!" Mom answered. "No matter how sinful we are, Jesus will always love us and wait for us to come to Him. The Bible says that He will never leave us nor forsake us."[20]

"But what will we do about Puff?" Sarah asked. "I heard her meowing so piteously at the door last night."

"I think Blackie also knows that Puff is not a mother anymore and

Learning Lessons From Furry Friends

that she dislikes the kittens. That's why Blackie chases Puff out of the garage to keep her away from her babies. Then Puff can't sleep in her warm box. We will have to give Puff lots of attention so that she knows we still love her."

The Browns did their best to give Puff attention, but she seemed to feel downright disgusted with the kittens. Soon Puff began disappearing for a couple days at a time, and then reappearing again to see if the  kittens were gone yet. This went on until the kittens had grown up and gone to new homes. The very day after the last kitten went home with its new owners, Puff brought a mouse and laid it on the Brown's doorstep as a thank offering!

Weeks, months, and years passed by. Neither Blackie nor Puff was young anymore. Seasons came and went. Another cold winter set in when Sarah was twelve years old. Snow lay in heaps everywhere, and the temperatures dropped far below zero. Blackie and Puff huddled together in their box in the garage listening to the coyotes' eerie howling on the hills beyond the woods.

One morning Sarah remarked to Mom, "Puff has been acting strange. She keeps meowing mournfully, but she doesn't want to be picked up or petted. It's like she's looking for something."

"Hmm." Mom kneaded her bread dough thoughtfully. "Have you been feeding the cats enough? Maybe Puff is hungry?"

"No, that can't be it, because there is always plenty of food left in their dish."

The Intruder

"Maybe Blackie's missing?" Mom interjected. "Have you seen her lately?"

Hosea came into the room just then. "Mom, I haven't seen Blackie since we came home from our Christmas trip, but I didn't say anything then because I thought she would have come home by now."

"That must be why Puff is crying," Sarah exclaimed. "I hope nothing happened to poor Blackie."

For days Puff called and called and cried for her mother, but Blackie never returned. Puff had lost her best friend and seemed heartbroken, while the coyotes' howls seemed to have a triumphant ring to them. In time Puff's hurt healed, and she soon was enjoying quiet days without any kittens to bother her.

But her days of solitude were coming to a close!

But her days of solitude were coming to a close!

Learning Lessons From Furry Friends

"Mom, I think we should get another kitty. It's been a while since we lost Blackie," seventeen-year-old Theodore stated. "Maybe the kitten could be mine; Sarah and Hosea have both had their own kitten."

"We'll have to talk to Dad first," Mom answered.

"I know some kittens we could choose from if he says yes," Sarah put in. "Some of the cutest calico kittens were born on our friend's farm."

"Really?" Theodore asked. "If we could just take Dad to see them, he'd realize how cute they are and would fall in love with them. Then he would let us bring one home."

"That's not a bad idea." Mom's eyes twinkled. "He really is softhearted when it comes to animals, even if he tries to deny it."

It worked! Daddy reluctantly went to see the kittens, but they quickly melted his heart, and it wasn't long before he gave his consent to bring one home. The little kittens had to stay on the farm with their mother for a few more weeks, but the day soon came when Theodore excitedly picked out his kitten. "I'll name her Smudge. With all her orange and black patches she looks like someone smudged paint on her fur," he explained on the way home.

Puff was not happy to see the new arrival. As Theodore carried the kitten into the house, she growled menacingly and glared at the "intruder" with angry green eyes. She seemed to have resolved to never let another cat take Blackie's place.

For the first few weeks, Smudge lived in the house, so she could get used to her new home. Then she would go outside for a few hours every nice day, and then for most of the day. Soon she was old enough to be outside all the time.

Puff seemed to have decided to ignore the new rival, but she soon found that Smudge would not be ignored. She seemed to enjoy spending

The Intruder

...she glared at the "intruder" with angry green eyes.

time with Puff, even though Puff treated her very coldly. If Puff was sitting placidly on the porch, Smudge would pad up in her quiet way and just sit silently next to her.

"She is so sweet to everyone!" Sarah declared to Mom. "She takes it for granted that everyone likes her, which usually is the case anyway."

Mom laughed, "Smudge is showing us the best way to make friends. The Bible says, 'A man who has friends must himself be friendly.'[21] Sometimes we must show love and friendship even to people who are mean and spiteful to us in return; eventually they may make some of the best friends we've ever had. Just wait and see, Smudge will find her way into Puff's heart sooner or later."

It wasn't too many days before Sarah came rushing excitedly into the house. "Guess what, Mom," she exclaimed. "Puff and Smudge are sleeping together in the same box!"

Learning Lessons From Furry Friends

"Really? That's wonderful!" Mom wrapped Sarah in a hug.

"Puff was lying there with the most sheepish look on her face, as if she was hoping that none of her other friends would see her sleeping with a little kitten!" Sarah couldn't keep from giggling.

Mom laughed. "Puff probably wouldn't admit it if you asked her, but she loves Smudge!"

"Yes," Sarah giggled. "I think I know how Smudge weaseled her way into Puff's box too! I can just imagine how it happened: Smudge was sitting on the table next to Puff's box while Puff was trying to ignore her and sleep. Pretty soon, one of Smudge's front paws was inside the box, then the other. All this was done very slowly, quietly, and casually while Smudge gazed innocently around the room. After a while, her back paws somehow slipped in. Before Puff knew it, Smudge was curled up next to her, licking her face. And Puff was

Oh, animals are such fun!

thinking, 'Well, maybe I like her a little bit after all.'" Mom and Sarah laughed until tears ran down their cheeks.

"Oh, animals are such fun!" Mom exclaimed, wiping her eyes. "They each have their own personality, just like people. There are so many things we can learn about ourselves just from observing them."

"If I had to name Puff's personality, it would probably be 'stuck up.' She walks around with her nose in the air, and everything must be precisely to her liking! But, really, that's what makes her so interesting." Sarah smiled.

"Smudge's personality, on the other hand, is the sweetest, friendliest, and most loving kitten we have ever had!" Mom stated.

Unfortunately, it was only a few months later that Smudge tried to follow the Browns on a walk. She slipped into the woods, climbed a tree, and never returned. Again Puff called and cried for many days, and everyone realized just how much she had really loved Smudge!

"Do you think we'll ever find out what happened to Smudge?" Sarah asked.

"Probably not," Mom answered. "It could be that another animal got her."

"Why do all these bad things happen to our kitties?" Sarah wondered. "I mean," she continued, "we've had kittens die, both Mama Kitty and Blackie disappeared, and now Smudge is gone."

"Everything has to end sometime, Sweetheart," Mother soothed, "even life itself. This life while we live it will bring us much happiness, but it will also bring much sorrow. You can't have one without the other. If we never had sad times, we would never appreciate the glad times."

Mom continued, "But we shouldn't dwell on all the sad things that happen to us in life. Instead, let's think of all the fun times we've had and all the valuable lessons we've learned!"

"Like teaching the kittens how to drink milk," Sarah broke in. "Isn't it cute the way kittens sputter and spit when they first stick their noses into the milk?"

"Yes," Mom laughed, "and like the time when you tied a gum wrapper on the end of a string and dragged it across the floor. Tuffy went creeping stealthily after it and then pounced on it viciously like it was a live mouse!"

"Oh, and like the time Blueberry tried to sneak up on Muffin, but just when she was getting ready to pounce on him, Tigger jumped on her from behind and scared her so much that she almost jumped out of her fur!" Sarah giggled at the memory.

"And we've learned so many things about raising and caring for animals that we could never relate them all! You see, Sarah," Mom pointed out, "I think there are many more happy times than sad times!"

"Yes," Sarah smiled, "and when I think about it, if we had never raised kittens—sure we might not have had to go through the hard times—but we would never have had any of these wonderful memories either. I wouldn't trade them for anything in the world!"

"And in heaven, there will never again be any sorrow, only everlasting joy!"[22] Mom gave Sarah a happy squeeze.

"O LORD, You preserve man and beast. How precious is Your lovingkindness, O God!"
(Psalm 36:6, 7).

Chapter 7

A New Pet

It was a beautiful April day! The sunshine danced on new, tender blades of grass while great, puffy clouds sailed lazily through the vast blue sky.

Sarah took a deep breath of fresh air as she stepped out of the house and shut the door. Hopping and skipping to the mailbox, she pulled out a stack of letters and papers and returned to the house, leafing through the pile to see if anything interesting had come.

The next morning everyone sat around the breakfast table eating Mom's yummy waffles.

"When are we going to get a new puppy?" Hosea wondered. "Tiree died last fall."

"Yeah," Sarah chimed in, "you said we could get a dog in the spring, Daddy!"

"I suppose we can start looking for a dog," Dad answered.

"Goody!" Sarah cried. "I'll get the newspaper; it came yesterday! What kind of dog should we get?" She jumped up from the table and rushed to grab the newspaper from Mom's desk.

Mom and Dad laughed at her exuberance. "You don't pick out a puppy all in one day," Mom told her with a smile.

"I know that," Sarah laughed, too, "but it doesn't hurt to start looking." She leafed through the papers until she came to the classified section.

"What breed of dog should we get?" Theodore asked.

A New Pet

"When I was a boy," Dad answered, "we had an American Water Spaniel. They are really quite smart. Maybe we could get one of those, or maybe a mix with one."

But it wasn't an American Water Spaniel that became the Brown family's newest member. It was a little black and white Border Collie. It happened this way:

Ring, ring! "I'll get it!" Sarah cried, running to pick up the phone. "Hello? Oh, hi Daddy! OK, here she is," Sarah handed the phone to Mother. As she listened to the one-sided conversation, she grew more and more excited.

"They had a sign out by the driveway?" Mom was asking. "Border Collie puppies! Aren't they usually farm dogs? ... Oh, so they make good family pets too. Well, that certainly is interesting! How many puppies does the lady have available? ... So you really like the black puppy with four white paws? ... Sure, Sarah and I can drive over there right away! ... You're sure you want a Border Collie puppy? ... OK, we'll be over soon! Bye!"

Mom had barely hung up the phone before Sarah exclaimed, "What did he say? Are we going to get a puppy? Are we going to drive over and see them right now?"

Mom laughed, "One question at a time! A lady had a sign out at the end of her driveway for Border Collie puppies. And you know how Daddy is; he went to see them and fell right in love with this little black and white puppy. Yes, you and I are going to drive to the lady's house and take a look at the puppies ourselves. That way, since Dad has to finish running his errands, we can bring the puppy home with us if we decide to get her."

"Oh, goody! We're getting a puppy; we're getting a puppy!" Sarah jumped up and down and raced to her room for a jacket and shoes. Soon

Learning Lessons From Furry Friends

It didn't take Mom and Sarah long to spot the little puppy that Dad had liked.

Mom and she were in the car headed toward the place where Sarah felt sure they would pick out their new pet.

When they arrived, the owner of the Border Collie puppies led them to a large kennel in the backyard and a chorus of excited yaps and barks greeted them. It didn't take Mom and Sarah long to spot the little puppy that Dad had liked.

"Oh, you're *so* cute!" Sarah exclaimed. "Do you want to come home with us and be our new puppy?" The little Border Collie waggled her tail and licked Sarah's hand. Sarah bent down to take the puppy in her arms. Suddenly she was holding a wriggling and squirming bundle of black fur, and she quickly put the puppy down. The puppy immediately ran with her tail tucked between her legs to her doghouse.

"What's the matter with her?" Sarah asked Mom.

"Oh, she must have gotten scared that you were going to take her away from her mommy," Mom answered with a smile.

Sarah laughed and hurried over to gently pull the puppy from the doghouse. Then she scooped her up in her arms and petted her until she calmed down.

"Can't we please take her home with us? She'd make a good doggie, I'm sure!" Sarah begged.

Mom, who never liked to make hasty decisions, had to think about it and talk with Daddy and the puppies' owner first, but she finally made up her mind! "This little dog is going to be the next addition to our family!" she decided with a smile.

However, the little puppy did not seem to be too happy about this new arrangement. First, she become nervous and sick to her stomach on the ride home and lost all her breakfast. After pulling into the driveway and giving Shasta a chance to go to the bathroom, Mom and Sarah took her into the house. She immediately spied the large dining room table in one corner and hurried to crawl underneath. Then she curled up and lay glaring at her new family.

Hosea crowded around the table beside Mom and Sarah. "Hi there, puppy!" he said. "What's wrong? Why don't you come out from under there and play?"

Learning Lessons From Furry Friends

"Don't worry," Mom explained with a smile, "she's just upset that we took her away from her mother. Let's leave her alone for a while, and she'll get over it soon enough." It didn't take long for the little dog to close her eyes and drift off to sleep.

Then she curled up and lay glaring at her new family.

The voices of Dad and Theodore arriving home awakened the new little puppy, but she wouldn't budge from her place under the table. "Mom said that she's mad because we took her away from her mommy," Sarah explained to Theodore.

"And she's probably a little scared and nervous, too, since she doesn't understand what's happening to her," Theodore assumed.

Dad knelt down and peered under the table. "Come on out here, you silly puppy!" he baby-talked as he playfully pulled her out from

A New Pet

under the table. Then he began scratching the little dog's ears, stroking her back, and rubbing her tummy. At first the puppy only hid her face between Dad's legs, but soon her tail began to wag, ever so slightly, and little by little her shyness wore away until she was playfully growling in mock anger when Daddy used his hand as a "spider" that crawled stealthily across the floor toward her feet.

The ice was broken, and the rest of the evening everyone had lots of fun playing with their new pet. Bedtime soon came, and the fun had to wait until morning to be continued. Sarah took the puppy outside one last time, and then put her to bed in a large box lined with a blanket. Daddy covered the box with a board to keep the pup from jumping out, and then he turned out the lights.

Pretty soon the little doggie noticed that everything was quiet and that she couldn't hear any of her new friends. Suddenly she felt very scared and lonely, so she whined and scratched at the side of her box. When no one came to get her, she howled. A light came on, and she perked up her ears as footsteps came down the hall. It was working!

Someone took the cover off the box, and there stood Dad, yawning. "Why, you're just fine!" he assured the puppy. "Now be quiet and go to sleep," he whispered, lightly squeezing her snout. He replaced the cover on her box and flipped off the lights.

The puppy tried to be quiet for a while, but the aching loneliness just wouldn't go away, and she started to whine and howl again. On went the lights… This went on for much of the night, and no one got much sleep. After that night, Dad allowed the puppy to sleep with Sarah until she grew big enough be outside all the time.

"What should we name our new puppy?" The question came up again and again the next day, but the result never seemed to change.

"I like the name Daisy!" Mom said.

Dad laughed and replied teasingly, "That reminds me of a cow!"

"Well, she is a Border Collie, and Border Collie's often herd cattle!"

"I want to name her Jasmine!" Sarah exclaimed.

"Or Princess!" Theodore put in.

Hosea thought for a moment and then said, "Let's not name her something too common—I mean, there are lots of dogs named Daisy, and Princess, and Lady. Let's think of something unique."

"Jasmine is unique!" Sarah reminded him. And on and on it went.

Finally, Mother had a wonderful idea for picking out a name. "Let's get out our trees and flowers card game and name our new puppy after a unique tree or flower." Everyone gathered in the living room as Mom read the names off the cards one by one.

"Well, what names do we have to choose from?" Dad asked Sarah, who had written down the ones that everyone liked.

"Let's see," she replied, "for trees everyone liked Ceiba, and everyone agreed that Gumbo-Limbo, Sycamore, and Fleebane were out of the question!" The family laughed together at the thought of calling their new puppy "Fleebane."

"Then for flowers. No one liked Black-eyed Susan or Clover except me," Sarah stated. "Mom likes Sweet Pea and Buttercup, but that reminds Dad of a cow again. The only ones everyone liked are: Lily,

A New Pet

Merry-bell, and Shasta Daisy." It took some discussion, but finally everyone unanimously decided to name the new puppy Shasta Daisy.

"It's such a pretty name!" Sarah expressed with a fond smile at little Shasta. "I'm so glad that Jesus found us a puppy to adopt! He knew all along that we would need a good doggie, and He picked Shasta beforehand, didn't He?"

"I'm sure He did, Sarah," Mom answered. "Jesus loves to answer the prayers of His children."

"Do you think He has any lessons for us to learn from Shasta?"

"I'm sure of it!" Mom smiled. "I can think of one right now. We adopted Shasta into our family just like the Lord adopts us into His family."

"What do you mean?" Sarah wondered.

Mom reached for her Bible. "Let me show you something amazing. In the Bible we are told that we can become sons and daughters of God. For example, Galatians 3:26 says, 'For you are all sons [and daughters] of God through faith in Christ Jesus.' John 1:12 also tells us that we can become children of God by believing on Jesus."

"But what did you mean by 'adopted'?" Sarah questioned, listening intently.

"Well, we aren't born into God's family, just like Shasta wasn't born into our family. Everyone is born as a sinner.[23] In that sense we all start out as children of the world, and not of God. We all need Jesus to save us from our sins. And when we allow Him to transform our lives and come into our hearts, He adopts us into His family, just like we adopted Shasta."

The light began to dawn on Sarah's face. "Oh, I see! But then what happens after we're adopted into His family?"

Mother thought for a moment. The she began leafing through the

Learning Lessons From Furry Friends

pages of her Bible. "Here's the answer to your question, Sarah-dear," she said after a moment of searching. "'Do all things without complaining and disputing, that you may become blameless and harmless, children of God without fault in the midst of a crooked and perverse generation, among whom you shine as lights in the world.' That's from Philippians 2:14, 15. This means that after we become adopted in the family of God we are to live in such a way that we will be lights to the world. In this way we will lead others into God's family."

"Well, I'm happy that Shasta's part of our family, but I'm even happier that I can be a part of God's family!" Sarah expressed.

Little Shasta, hearing her name, looked up at Sarah and waggled her tail, as if to say, "I think so too!"

"Behold what manner of love the Father has bestowed on us, that we should be called children of God!" (1 John 3:1).

A New Pet

Chapter 8

Puppies

Weeks and months passed, and Shasta soon latched onto her new family with all her heart. She proved to be very intelligent, as she quickly learned to come, sit, stay, and heel. The Browns worked with Shasta a lot, and soon she knew many tricks like "Roll over," "Sit up," "Speak," "Howl," "Shake paws," and "Beg."

Sometimes the children made mistakes and would yell at Shasta or handle her a little roughly if she didn't do what they wanted. But over time they learned better training methods. It didn't take long to realize that a dog is more apt to obey if its owner is patient and calm. Then the dog will *want* to please its owner.

The Brown family made many happy memories with Shasta. Playing fetch was one of her favorite activities. She would have played for hours on end if someone in the family could have lasted that long. Shasta also loved to run, and the older she got the faster she got, until she could race right alongside the kids as they flew down the road on their bikes.

Puppies

Shasta knew many tricks like 'Roll over,' 'Sit up,' 'Speak,' 'Howl,' 'Shake paws,' and 'Beg.'

Shasta loved Puff, but Puff did not love Shasta! "Shasta never hurts Puff, but she sometimes teases her too much!" Sarah explained during one meal.

"Yeah, I've watched Shasta paw at Puff, trying to get her to run so she could frantically chase after her," Theodore said.

"But Puff must like Shasta a little bit, or she wouldn't snuggle up to her in the doghouse like she did last night," Dad proposed. "Besides, sometimes I think it's a game they both play with each other—Shasta teasing Puff, and Puff pretending to be so scared that she has to scramble away from Shasta."

Everyone smiled. "You could be right," Mom affirmed. "But one thing is certain; Shasta has really grown to love us and our home."

A year passed since the Browns had brought Shasta home, and they had an exciting idea. "Wouldn't it be fun to have puppies with Shasta?" Mom asked enthusiastically.

"She'd be a really good mother!" Sarah exclaimed.

"We could find new homes for the puppies easily since Border Collies make good farm dogs and are very smart," Dad interjected.

And so it was that Shasta found herself one day on her way to meet her new "husband," who turned out to be a very sweet-tempered male Border Collie. His owners were very kind, and Shasta stayed with them for several days.

After she came home again, changes began to take place inside her as six little puppies were developing and growing in her womb. In a little over a month, her bulging tummy gave ample evidence to her pregnancy, as well as the fact that she had gotten very slow and could barely keep up on walks.

After another month, one day while Shasta was napping on the porch, Sarah came skipping out of the house carrying a pile of blankets. She took them into the garage and ran happily back into the house. Soon Dad came out with a board and some tools. Shasta looked on curiously at the bustle of activity. She waddled after Daddy into the garage and watched as he used the board to wall in a nook between an old wood stove and work table. Mom and Sarah came out then with big sheet of plastic that they began to spread out on the floor in the nook, all the while talking and laughing.

Shasta cocked her head, observing all this strange activity with wonderment. Sarah noticed her confused expression and giggled. "We're making you a bed, silly old pup, for you to have your puppies in." Sarah grabbed one of the blankets, and Mom took the other, and they both fluffed them up in the bed.

"There!" exclaimed Mom. "All finished!"

"Shasta, come and see if you like your new bed for your babies," Sarah called, kneeling beside the nest and patting the blankets. Shasta hopped in and curled up in the softness and coziness. "She likes it!" Sarah squealed delightedly. Shasta wagged her tail and gave Sarah a kiss to show how pleased she was.

Later on that week, Sarah remarked to Mother, "Shasta spends so much time curled up in her box! It seems like she only comes out to eat and go to the bathroom."

"That's because she senses that the time is near for her puppies to be born," Mom answered with a smile. "You just wait and see. She'll

Learning Lessons From Furry Friends

Soon everyone was crowded around, gazing at the babies.

probably give birth any day now."

One night, hours after the house was dark and quiet and everyone was sound asleep, Shasta began to feel uneasy. The moon shone brightly and the breeze blew warmly, just as normal. Still, something inside of her was telling her that the time had come for her puppies to be born.

That "something" was her instinct. At creation God gave the animals and birds an instinct to impress them how and when to do things. For example, geese are impressed through their instincts when to fly south for the winter, and other animals are impressed how to care for their young.

She kicked her blankets into a pile, and then nestled into them. Soon great waves of pain engulfed her, but she did not cry out, since pain is just part of giving birth. Soon a puppy appeared, and she quickly licked it clean and dry, urging it to suck some warm milk. Then she curled around her sweet baby to keep her warm and waited for the next one to be born. This happened five more times until Shasta was contentedly gazing at her six beautiful puppies.

The sun was just peeking over the horizon when Sarah ambled into the garage, yawning and rubbing her eyes. "Hi, Shasta," she yawned, "did you have any puppies last—" Sarah stopped short and stared. Then, forgetting that most of the household was still asleep, she excitedly ran back inside. "They're born, they're born! The puppies are here!" she cried, waking the sleepy family. Soon everyone was crowded around, gazing at the babies.

The teenaged boys yawned, rubbed their eyes sleepily, and said, "Oh. Nice." Then they ambled back to bed. However, Sarah and Mom stayed for a long time beside Shasta, wide awake and enchanted by the new arrivals.

During those first few days, Sarah was a very regular visitor to the garage, coming in every few hours to check on Shasta and her puppies. Shasta, too, hardly dragged herself away from them, only leaving to eat or go to the bathroom. Sometimes Mom would come with Sarah, and the two of them would just sit and gaze at the little puppies as they suckled the warm milk from their mother.

"Shasta, you are a very blessed mommy to have such a cute, healthy family!" Mom stroked the Border Collie's head.

"There are two males—one blue and white and the other black and white—and four females—another blue and white and the rest black and white," Sarah informed her.

Mother nodded. "Shasta's such a good mother. See how careful she is not to lay on any of her puppies, and she makes sure to regularly lick them when they are nursing."

"Why does she have to lick them?" Sarah wondered.

Learning Lessons From Furry Friends

"When puppies are still newborns, they can't go to the bathroom themselves," Mom replied, "so God planned for the mother dog to lick them in order to keep their bed and their bodies clean."

"She must love them a lot!" Sarah exclaimed. "She makes sure they are always safe! Sometimes when they are sleeping, she leaves the bed and walks around the yard to see that all is well and that her puppies aren't in danger."

"And remember when she barked last night?" Mom asked. "She probably heard a strange noise, and she was guarding her babies from larger animals that might attempt to harm them, or from people that she thinks might injure them.

"The neatest thing about this is the fact that Shasta has never had a litter of puppies before," Mom went on. "She doesn't have a doctor to tell how to take of her babies, but yet she knows just what to do! That's because the Lord is impressing her through her instincts."

"How come people don't have instincts?" Sarah was always full of questions.

"That is a good question, Sweetheart." Mom smiled at her daughter. "That is one of the things that sets humans apart from any other creature. The Lord did not create people with instincts. He created them with the power to choose for themselves. He will never force anyone to do what is right. But the Lord gave us two things to help us make choices. First, He gave each one of us a conscience. This is the part of our brain that discerns right from wrong. The Bible tells us that our conscience will prompt us to leave behind shameful practices, dishonesty, and falsehood.[24]

"Second, the Lord promised to send us the Holy Spirit. The Bible speaks of the Holy Spirit as a 'still small voice.'[25] It is sort of like hearing a little voice in your head saying, 'This is the right thing to do … this is the happy way … don't do what you know to be wrong.'[26] If we listen to the still small voice and compare its promptings to what the Bible says, we will never go wrong, for that is how the Lord Himself shows us the choices that will lead to life in heaven with Him."[27]

Mom was quiet for a moment, and then she put her arm around Sarah and asked her, "Have you made the choice to serve Jesus with all your heart?" Sarah nodded her head solemnly.

Have you, dear reader, made the choice to serve Jesus? If you haven't, you can do it right now by praying this prayer: "Dear Jesus, I know You love me and want to be My friend. Thank You for dying on the cross for my sins so I can live. I want to make the choice now to live for You. Please help me! I love you! Amen."

"Choose for yourselves this day whom you will serve … But as for me and my house, we will serve the LORD" (Joshua 24:15).

Chapter 9

Teaching and Learning

With God's help and through Shasta's tender, loving care, the little puppies began to grow bigger and started to nurse longer and less often. In order to nourish herself as well as her puppies, Shasta began to gobble down large amounts of dog food. God created her body with the ability to use part of the food she ate to nourish herself and make the other part into milk for her puppies.

When her puppies were born, their eyes were tightly closed and their ears were sealed shut. God formed them in the womb this way so

As their legs grew stronger, they started to play with each other.

Teaching and Learning

that the tiny parts inside the eyes and ears could develop completely before being used. But within about two weeks, their eyes and ears were fully open.

"I've finally thought of names for all the puppies," Sarah announced one day soon after the puppies' eyes had opened. "They are Ashes, Britches, Daisy, Blacky, Button, and Rotunda, since she's so roly-poly," Sarah giggled. "Now it'll be easier to know which puppy I'm talking about since they all have names."

The puppies became more and more confident over the next few days and began to try out their shaky legs. As their legs grew stronger, they started to play with each other.

"It's so much fun to watch the puppies now!" Sarah exclaimed to Mother. "One will playfully bite the other, and the other will give a little growl in return. This morning," Sarah laughed, "oh, you should have seen it, Mom! Little Daisy and Blacky were fighting. Daisy stood up on her back legs to paw at Blacky's face, but Blacky rammed herself into Daisy, and Daisy lost her balance and fell over backward onto Ashes. Well, that scared him to pieces! You should have heard him squeal!" Sarah and Mom laughed.

"All this play-fighting is good for the puppies as well as entertaining," Mom informed Sarah. "God intended for puppies to playfully fight for a couple of reasons," she explained. "It helps their muscles and legs grow stronger, and it also prepares them to know how to defend themselves if a wild animal were to attack them."

At the age of three weeks,

as the puppies' muscles grew stronger from playing harder, they began to need more nourishment than Shasta could give them through her milk. The time had come for them to have their first taste of solid food. Sarah prepared a pan of dog food softened with warm milk and brought it out to them. They sniffed hungrily at it and then hastily gobbled it down. From then on they ate a pan of softened dog food twice a day and grew rapidly from the good nourishment.

The pups had grown quite a bit in the four weeks since they were born, and the bed in the garage was getting quite crowded. Another problem was that the puppies, since they were eating heartily of dog food, left much more waste than Shasta could clean up and, as a result, their bed became quite dirty.

Thereafter, the pups spent most of their days in a small round pen in the warm sunshine on the back lawn. Sarah placed a board over the top of the small pen to discourage large birds, such as hawks, owls, or eagles, from stealing a puppy for dinner. Then she and Mom cleaned out the bed in the garage to be used only at nighttime.

Sarah spent much of her time playing with the puppies or holding them in her lap. But when Mom came out of the house to do some weeding in the garden, she noticed that Sarah seemed to be having a hard time with the puppies.

"It doesn't look like you are having much fun!"

"How can I when the puppies tug on my dress, run away from me when I go to pick them up, or chew on my ankles! *Ouch*!" Britches had nipped Sarah on the ankle.

"God planned for puppies to have training just like little children. It's not good to let a puppy bite or jump on you. Just as children need to learn good manners, puppies also need to learn to come and sit on command," Mother explained. "You must give the puppies correction if they do not obey immediately. Say 'no' and give them a squeeze on their snout if they should bite you. Proper training over time will make the puppies easier to work with and more fun to play with."

Mom was right, and even Shasta knew that her puppies needed more training. One day Sarah came flying into the house, crying that Shasta was hurting her puppy. "She rolled Ashes on his back and bit him on the neck!"

Mom calmly followed Sarah back outside and then explained with a smile, "You see, Shasta is training her puppies too. She's making sure they understand that she is in charge. Perhaps Ashes was biting Shasta or trying to dominate her by not respecting her authority. Shasta was only making Ashes submit by putting him on his back and giving nips of correction. She wasn't trying to injure him, but she wants Ashes to know that he must obey."

Mom went on, "Shasta also teaches the pups through play. She's taught them to defend themselves from wild animals by playfully fighting with them. But most importantly, she is teaching them how to get along nicely with each other and socialize well with other dogs. God planned for the puppies to learn their most important lessons from

Learning Lessons From Furry Friends

their mother's training and from spending time with their littermates."

Sarah thought for a moment. "The puppies will soon be eight weeks old. When are we going to find new homes for them? Some people sell their puppies when they are six weeks old, you know."

"Yes, some people do," Mom answered. "You see, six weeks old is right around the time that puppies start to teethe and chew on things. They can be very destructive at times, and it seems that people get tired of that and want to get rid of them. Still, it's not a good idea to sell them that young."

"What do you mean?" Sarah questioned.

"I think that all puppies should stay with their mothers until they are *at least* eight weeks old. Think how much they could learn from Shasta in two weeks."

"I see what you mean!" Sarah exclaimed. "Shasta is still teaching her puppies many valuable things, and if they left now, at six to seven weeks old, they never would learn those good things!"

"That's right. You know, learning is a very important thing," Mom mused. "Not just for puppies, but for people too."

"Do you mean *learning* as in *school*?" Sarah wrinkled her nose.

"Partly," Mom replied. "One of the best ways to learn is in school. But learning does not mean just reading, writing, and numbers. Even after a young person finishes school he or she still goes on learning. In fact, we will each keep on learning until the day we die. What do you think is the best thing you can learn?" Mom questioned Sarah with a smile.

Teaching and Learning

Sarah thought for a moment. "Math? Daddy said a person needs math skills to do anything in life."

"He's right; math skills are essential. But the learning I'm talking about is even better than that. It is a knowledge that will last for eternity."

"Oh, I know!" Sarah exclaimed. "The best thing you can learn about is Jesus and the Bible!"

"Very good!" Mom praised. "Jesus says in the Bible, 'Take My yoke upon you and learn from Me.'[28] The Bible also tells us that knowledge and understanding are even more important that great riches.[29] And while it's possible for a person to spend too much time learning from books,[30] you can never learn too much about God and the Bible. It's not even possible to learn half of what there is to know about Him."[31]

"I guess there's a lot more I can learn about this world and about God," Sarah stated, "just like there's a lot more for the puppies to learn from Shasta."

The puppies did learn a lot from Shasta in the next two weeks, and Sarah was glad they had waited to find new homes for them. Anyway, she wanted to spend as much time with the sweet little puppies as she could before they went to new owners. The time flew by too quickly, however, and soon Mom had put an ad in the newspaper for the little Border Collie puppies.

Soon after that, all the precious pups went to homes, and the days that follows seemed quiet and empty. "It makes me both happy and sad," Sarah remarked to Mother. "I really miss those cute little puppies, but at the same time, I'm glad to be able to relax now. They took up a lot of time!"

"I know!" Mom agreed. "But we will always have our memories, and no one can take away the lessons we learned and the knowledge we gained. We can always be thankful that God has given us this opportunity to work with His creatures!"

Dear reader, giving your heart to Jesus marks, not the end, but the very beginning of your journey with Him. Read and study your Bible prayfully every day, and each time you will learn more of Jesus' love and care for you. It will not always be easy, but it will be a journey you won't regret—a journey that will last for all eternity!

"Search the Scriptures ... these are they which testify of Me" (John 5:39).

Endnotes

1. Mark 13:33
2. Matthew 24
3. Luke 21:34
4. Numbers 32:23
5. Revelation 1:5
6. Colossians 3:20
7. 1 Peter 5:8
8. Romans 8:28
9. Genesis 1:31
10. Romans 5:12
11. Revelation 21:4
12. Isaiah 11:6
13. Matthew 10:29
14. Matthew 10:31
15. Jeremiah 31:3
16. Romans 5:8
17. Job 1:21
18. Psalm 13:3
19. Ecclesiastes 9:5
20. Hebrews 13:5
21. Proverbs 18:24
22. Isaiah 35:10; 51:11
23. Psalm 51:5
24. 2 Corinthians 4:2
25. 1 Kings 19:12
26. Isaiah 30:21
27. John 16:13
28. Matthew 11:29
29. Proverbs 8:10
30. Ecclesiastes 12:12
31. Philippians 4:7

We invite you to view the complete
selection of titles we publish at:

www.TEACHServices.com

or write or email us your praises,
reactions, or thoughts about this
or any other book we publish at:

TEACH Services, Inc.
PUBLISHING

www.TEACHServices.com

P.O. Box 954
Ringgold, GA 30736

info@TEACHServices.com

TEACH Services, Inc., titles may be purchased in bulk for
educational, business, fund-raising, or sales promotional use. For information, please
e-mail
BulkSales@TEACHServices.com.

Finally, if you are interested in seeing
your own book in print, please contact us at

publishing@teachservices.com.

We would be happy to review your manuscript for free.